MAD For Kicks

Edited by

Albert B. Feldstein

A Warner Communications Company

WARNER BOOKS EDITION

For information address E.C. Publications, Inc.,
485 Madison Avenue, New York, N.Y. 10022

ISBN 0-446-98461-2

This Warner Books Edition is published by
arrangement with E.C. Publications, Inc.

Designed by Thomas Nozkowski

Warner Books, Inc.,
75 Rockefeller Plaza,
New York, N.Y. 10019

 A Warner Communications Company

Printed in the United States of America

First Printing: June, 1980

10 9 8 7 6 5 4 3 2 1

AND THE BOND PLAYS ON DEPT.

ALTHOUGH THE STARS KEEP CHANGING, "JAMES BOMB" MOVIES GO ON FOREVER! AND SO, MAD TURNS ITS SATIRICAL SPOTLIGHT ON THIS BOX OFFICE PHENOMENON, AND BRINGS ITS READERS UP TO DATE ON . . .

8 "JAMES BOMB" BOMB MOVIES

A MAD RETROSPECT ...WITH NO RESPECT

ARTIST: MORT DRUCKER · WRITER: ARNIE KOGEN

YES, NOSTALGIA FANS! REMEMBER YEARS AGO, WHEN THE "JAMES BOMB" MANIA FIRST SWEPT THE COUNTRY AND EVERYBODY WAS RUNNING TO SEE

"DR. NO-NO"

James Bomb! Call for James Bomb! Message for James Bomb!

I'LL take it, Son!

Is that **THE** James Bomb?

Yes . . . the **famous Secret Agent** with the incredible knowledge of **women, food,** and especially **wine!** I understand that he can not only tell you the **vineyard** and **year**—but also the name of the **gal** who stomped the **grapes!**

Waiter, I'd like a **Chateau Nov ka Pop 1951,** stomped by **Fat Harriet La Clutz!**

I'm **very sorry,** Sir! We're all out of **wine!**

Then I'll have a **dry Martini** . . . 6 parts **gin,** 1 part **vermouth,** 1 dash of **bitters . . . shaken gently** with **ice, NOT stirred . . .** and strained into a **large cocktail glass** with a **green olive!**

I'm **terribly sorry,** Sir . . . but we're out of **ALL alcoholic beverages!**

Hmmm! Then give me a **Fresca** in a **non-returnable bottle . . . chilled well** . . . with **no ice . . .** and **two straws!**

I don't **believe** it! James Bomb . . . drinking **FRESCA?!?**
You **forgot!** These **first** James Bomb movies were made on **very low budgets!**
What a **man!** He's **ruthless** . . . yet **suave!**
They say he has a **"License to Kill"!**
He **also** has a **"Learner's Permit to Make Out"!**
I know! The English don't mind **violence,** but they're rather **stuffy** about **SEX!**

You **sent** for me, Sir . . . ?
Yes, 007! Frygg, our Agent in Jamaica, has **vanished mysteriously!** I want you to go there and **investigate!** Can you leave **immediately?**
Of course, Sir! I **travel light!** All I need are my **gun** and my **wit!**
I've **HEARD** your wit! Yes—you **DO** travel light!
HQ
SECRET SERVICE SECRET
007
Good-bye, Mr. Bomb, and **do** take care!
I will, Mr. Pennymoney!
That's **MISS** Pennymoney! Oh, **James!** Look at me! I'm a **woman** . . . and I'm secretly **in love** with you! Why do you keep on **ignoring** me?!?
Keep on ignoring **WHO?**
See what I **mean?!**
Excuse me, Sir, but I'm in a **hurry!**
James, **why** do you always treat me like a **MAN?**
BECAUSE, my dear Pennymoney, compared to the girl in the **next scene,** you **ARE** a man!
N
WANTED FINGERPRINT

Hi! I'm Honey Roper . . . one of the exciting new discoveries you'll be seeing in these James Bomb films!
Wrong! TWO of the exciting new discoveries!
Actually, in real life, I'm Ursula Undress, and except for this part, my acting career has been a big nothing!
Don't sweat it! That same thing happened to someone very close to me! Mainly, ME!
Where are we?
This is the island of the master criminal, Dr. No-No!
But it looks deserted! Where is he?
It's Wednesday . . . the Doctor's day off! He's taking time out from maiming, torturing and killing to relax and play golf!
DRUCKER

At last we meet! I am Dr. No-No!
I'm James Bomb . . . and after two nights on your island with me, this is now Miss Yes-Yes!
You like my little home? That fish tank cost me three million dollars!
Boy! You have some thriving practice! The "Acupuncture" business must be booming!!
I am not a Medical Doctor, Bomb! I am a Scientist! A MAD Scientist, who plans to blow up North America! But before I do that, I have an ingenious scheme to torture you with my metal hand!
And what is that?
I am going to snip all your witty lines out of the script!
Tie them up!!
NO
NO
Amazing, Bomb! You not only escaped from a foolproof cell, crawled through a flooded ventilator shaft, ran through fire, throttled forty of my guards, slipped into a disguise undetected, blew up my laboratory and saved the Free World, but you are now throwing me to my death! How do you manage to DO all these things?
Magnificently . . . of course!
REACTO

"FROM RUSSIA WITH LUNACY"

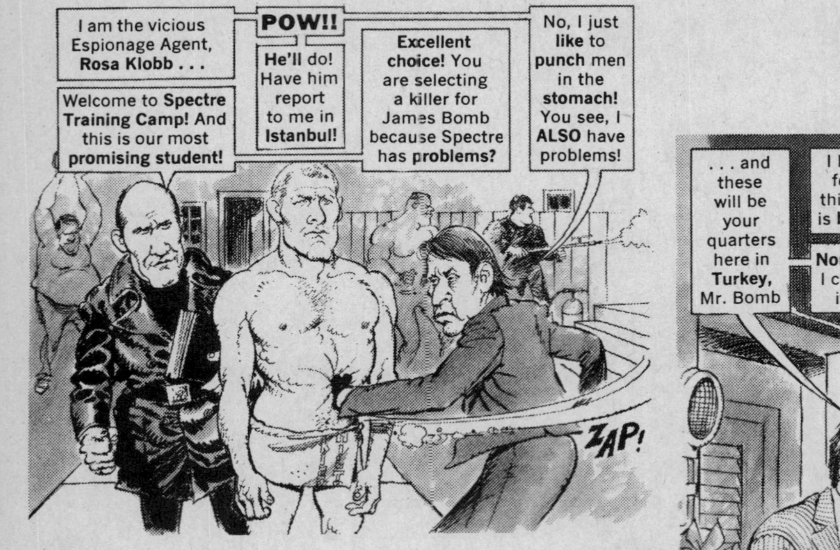
I am the vicious Espionage Agent, **Rosa Klobb . . .**
Welcome to **Spectre Training Camp!** And this is our most **promising student!**
POW!!
He'll do! Have him report to me in **Istanbul!**
Excellent choice! You are selecting a killer for James Bomb because Spectre has **problems?**
No, I just **like** to **punch** men in the **stomach!** You see, I **ALSO** have problems!
ZAP!
. . . and these will be your quarters here in **Turkey,** Mr. Bomb
I have a feeling this room is **bugged!**
Nonsense! I checked it out!
Good! I'm hungry! Can I call **Room Service?**
Surely! Just speak into the **lamp!**
Hmm! By the way, what did you say was the **name** of this hotel . . . ?
The Istanbul Watergate!

Bomb, I'm going to **strangle** you with the **wire device** encased in my **lethal wristwatch!**
Not before I kill you with my **exploding attaché case!**
In **that** case, I'll just **beat** you to death with my **fists!**
FISTS?!? What **are** you . . . some kind of **sickie??**
You've destroyed all my **underlings,** Bomb! So now you force me to kill you **myself** with my **poisoned shoe . . . spiked**
It won't work! I'm wearing my **arsenic-tipped golashes** to **counteract it!**
You're **too clever** for me, Bomb . . .
For **YOU, maybe!** But get a load of the **fat, shrewd villain** in my **next** movie, called—

"GOLDFINGERBOWL"

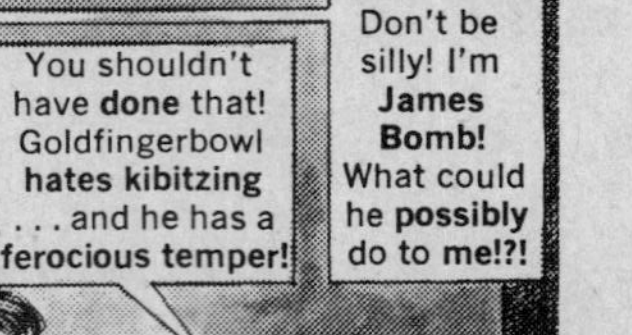

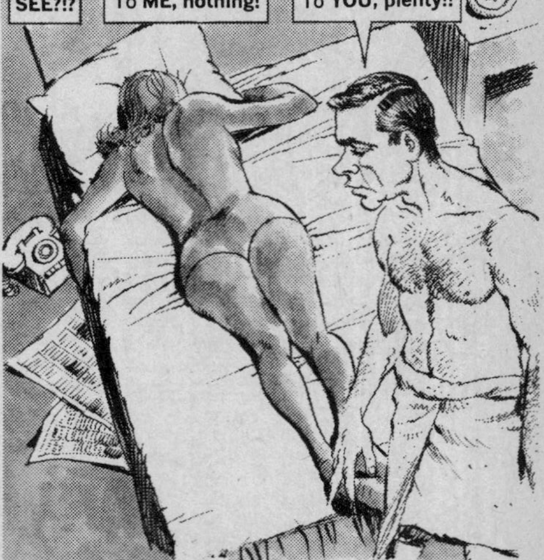

Oddblob, **tip your hat** to Mr. Bomb!
This is my fanatic manservant, **Oddblob!**
AMAZING! He's the **Sandy Koufax** of the **Derbies!**
That's **nothing!** When he **really** gets angry, you should see the terrible things he does with his **UNDERWEAR!!**
I hate to **do** this Chum, but—**'Bye!**
What **gadgets** on this Aston Martin! The **smoke screen,** the **oil slick,** the **twin machine guns** . . . and now **THIS**—the **ejector seat!** Too bad the heap only gets **six miles** to the **gallon!**
PHFFFT!
Why? You're only one of Goldfinger-bowl's **thugs!**
I could have **helped** you on that, Bomb! Now you and your kind will live to **regret** this!
No . . . I'm **Ralph Nader!**

You're becoming a **nuisance,** Bond! Tell me what you know about **"Operation Grand Slam"**!
Hah!! Do you **REALLY** expect me to **talk,** Goldfingerbowl??
Oh, **you'll** talk, all right! And if the laser beam **continues moving** as it is, you'll talk in a **very high-pitched voice!**
I'm **Tushy Galore,** and I'm a **Judo expert!**
You force me to **beat you up,** Tushy Galore!
Because I work for **Goldfingerbowl?**
No . . . because people are walking out of theaters all over the world talking about **YOUR** name, not **MINE** . . . and I have an **incredible ego!**

See that building?! Right there is the biggest gold supply in the Free World!
That's Fort Knox?!?
No, that's the offices of Crockoli and Saltzpeter . . . the Producers . . . who are making a mint ripping off the public with ludicrous movies like this one!
Fort Knox is a little further on!

. . . and that's my plan, Bomb! I will destroy the gold supply stored in Fort Knox, and turn the American economy into complete and utter chaos!
Why go to all that trouble? Why not just WAIT a few years . . . until President Nixon announces his Phase I through Phase IV Price Control Programs?!? You want chaos . . . THAT'S chaos!

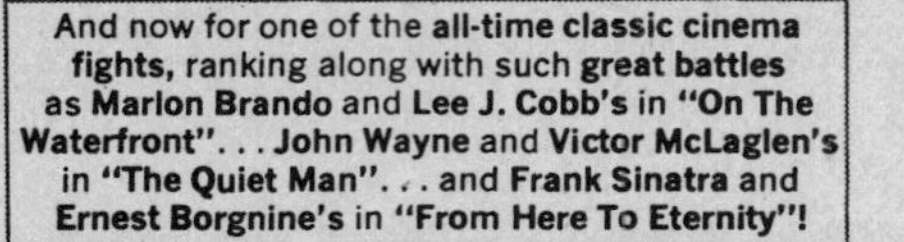
And now for one of the all-time classic cinema fights, ranking along with such great battles as Marlon Brando and Lee J. Cobb's in "On The Waterfront". . . John Wayne and Victor McLaglen's in "The Quiet Man". . . and Frank Sinatra and Ernest Borgnine's in "From Here To Eternity"!
Actually, it's more like Kitty trying to take on Matt Dillon in "Gunsmoke"!

Hope you get a "charge" out of this, Oddblob! That's one of my "current" jokes!
Please! Enough! Enough!
Enough electric shock?
No, the shock I rather like! Enough clever dialogue!
Sorry . . . but the clever dialogue will have to carry us through the next few pictures, because we're starting to un thin on gimmicks!
Not yet! Next is probably the most spectacular, but probably the DULLEST one of all—

"THUNDEBLAHH"

That James Bond may be a brilliant Agent on **land** . . . but this underwater assignment seems to be a bit **too much** for him!
What makes you say **that?**
He just **torpedoed** two tuna, **punched** a flounder and made a **witty, offhand remark** to a herring!
Well, James, you finally **killed** the villain **Lardo, recovered** the two missing **atom bombs,** smashed the **Spectre operation,** and now you've ended up in this **boat, alone** with **me!** So . . . **let's celebrate** in your **usual fashion . . .**
Dominique, you won't **believe** this, but I'm not in the **mood** for love!
Not in the **mood?** But you ate a **dozen oysters!**
Only **six** of them **worked!**
Is there **another girl . . . ?**
Yes! And **WE** wind up in a boat, **too,** at the end of . . .

"YOU ONLY LIVE NICE"

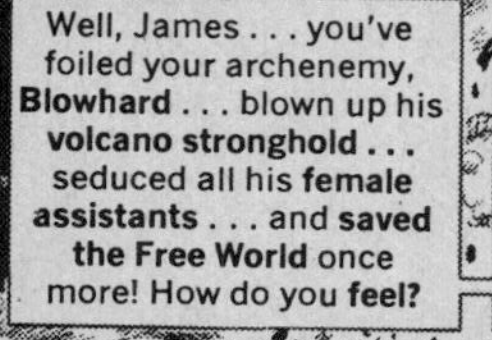

"ON HIS MAJESTY'S SECRET SHAMUS"

What a **fantastic film** this is turning out to be! I get to go to **Switzerland** and play **games** with **beautiful girls** . . .

. . . and finally, I get to meet the **evil, dangerous** and **fiendishly clever adversary** who has been trying to **kill** me all during the picture!
That's **right,** James Bomb! And now, it's **curtains** for you! Because you have caused me too much **trouble, embarrassment,** and a considerable loss of **income!** Not to mention **sex!**
CREW
LTD.

Sean Crockery! YOU!!
Yes! You've had an **incredible 90-minute career,** Lazybee! But now, **I'M** ready to take over the James Bond role again in—

"DOLLARS ARE FOREVER"

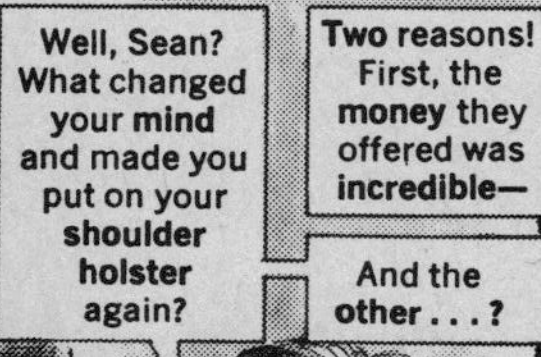

Say! You're Jill St. Joe, the gal who dates Henry Kissingfool, aren't you!?
That's right!
Tell me, how do I ccmpare to him?
Well, he's sexy!
I'M sexy!
He's very witty . . . and charming!
I'M very witty . . . and charming!
He has a brilliant future ahead of him!
I'M very witty . . . and charming!
Hurry!! It's hanging by a thin thread!
The rope?
No . . . my career!
Please!! Allow me to end that career, and start MINE . . . in

"LIVE AND LET SUFFER"

I guess it wasn't **funky** enough!
What do the **Tarot Cards** tell you about him, Canasta?
The cards tell me that he will cause you no **problems!**
Groovy! What **else** do they tell you?
They tell me that **President Nixon** did not know about **Watergate** . . . that there is **no Mafia** . . . that **Howard Cosell** is **modest** . . . and that **Totie Fields** will be the **next Miss America!**
I think we're in **big trouble!** We'd better **blow** Harlem and return to the **Caribbean!**

You're a dead man, Bomb! In a few minutes, you'll be torn to pieces! Would you believe that very alligator tore off my arm?
Sounds like a CROC to me!
Uggh! Oooff! You-you've overpowered me, Bomb! What a cultural switch! A White Man beating up a Black in a modern film!
It's a form of sweet revenge!
For the Secret Agents we killed? For subjecting your girlfriend to the pain of Voodoo torture?
No, tor the Box Office success of Black Movies like "Shaft"!

Roger Morbid, you've done **well** in the role of James Bomb!
Thank you, Sir!
You've done **so** well, you're going to be in the **next** James Bomb film, **"The Man With The Golden Gum"!**
Why, **thank** you, Sir!
And after that, we're going to do a version of James Bomb's great **UNDERWATER adventure, "For Fish Eyes Only"!**
With **ME,** of course!
No, I'm **afraid not!** You'll be **too old** and **too fat** by then! We're bringing in a **NEW young star!** One with the **acting talent necessary** for the role!
glugg glugg
MARK SPITZ INC.

DON MARTIN DEPT.

ONE EVENING AT HOME

KLIK
GLINK

EDNA! THAT'S DISGUSTING!!

You only got **one** out of **five**!!

You'll **never** make the **State Finals** with **that** kind of shooting!!

WOMENS
TOENAIL
CLIPPING
TEAM
1973

D. MARTIN.

BERG'S-EYE VIEW DEPT.

THE LIGHTER SIDE OF...

THE ENERGY CRISIS

ARTIST & WRITER: DAVE BERG

THIS IS A STICK-UP!!
Ha! I sure fooled you!
Yeah, heh-heh! You're always kidding around! I—uh—just came in for a little gas! Got any?
Sure! All the gas you want! For a DOLLAR a GALLON! And I ain't kiddin' around now!!
A—a DOLLAR a GALLON?!
THIS IS A STICK-UP!!

I think this so-called gas shortage is a big phony!

The big oil companies invented the whole thing so they could raise prices and make a killing!

Those dirty *&¢%$#@! CROOKS!!
WHOLESALE
MEATS
GOUGER& Co.
97-RT

What in heck is this country coming to? There are shortages of everything!

I freeze in Winter because there's a shortage of heating oil! I can't cool off in Summer because there's a shortage of electric power! I can't drive my car or boat because there's a shortage of gasoline. . . !

There's only one thing left that I can do! I'm going to the "Reading Room." . . !
You can forget that, too!
PLAYBOY

There's also a shortage of TOILET PAPER!

Here's a room with nobody in it! Yet the LIGHTS are on! The last one out of a room should shut the lights off!!

It's only EIGHTY DEGREES outside! We can certainly do without the Air Conditioner!

I must say, your husband is very diligent about saving watts! I'd call him a "GOOD CITIZEN"!
He was always this way!

Only BEFORE the energy crisis, you would have called him "CHEAP"!!

In accordance with the Divorce Decree, you must now divide up your community property! First, there's the RCA Color TV . . .
I want it!
No, I want it!

Next there's the Fisher Stereo Hi-Fi Equipment!
That's mine!
The heck it is!

NICKS
NO GAS
AL's
NO GAS
NO GAS

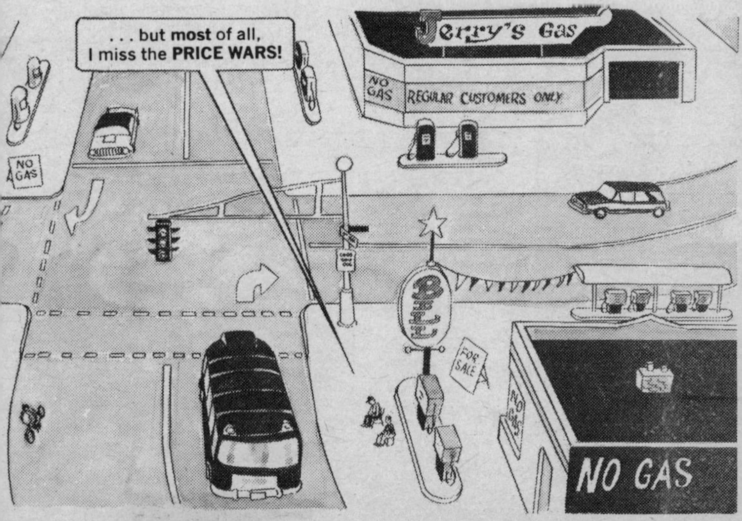

. . . but most of all, I miss the PRICE WARS!

Jerry's Gas

NO GAS

REGULAR CUSTOMERS ONLY

NO GAS

FOR SALE

NO GAS

NO GAS

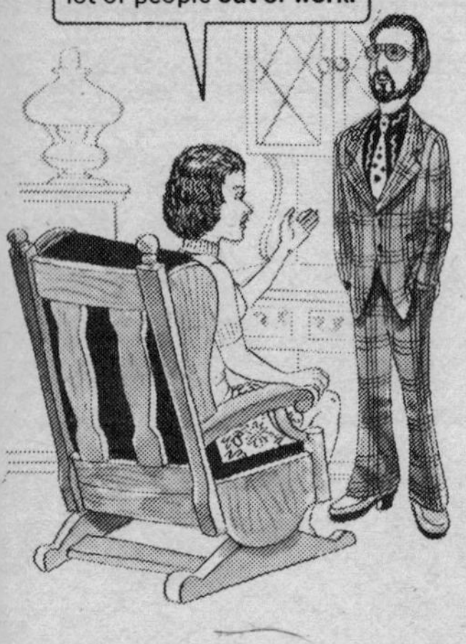
Boy, this oil shortage is **hurting!** It's putting a lot of people **out of work!**

Truck drivers, gas station attendants, airline pilots, toll booth collectors, auto workers, plastics extruders and all the **other** people that depend on oil!

There's **one thing GOOD** you can say about the oil shortage! There are lot less **accidents** on the highways!

See?!? It's even putting **HOSPITAL PERSONNEL** out of work!!

What are you . . . some kind of unpatriotic subversive?
Who, ME?
NY

Yes, YOU!! Our country is in the middle of a severe crisis! And what do you do?
NY

You drive around in a BIG GAS-EATING AMERICAN-MADE CAR

I can't believe what **happened** to me! Somebody just **siphoned** all the **gas** out of my tank!

Yeah! There's a **lot** of that **going around. . .!**

You'd better sell me a cap with a **lock** for my gas tank!

Sorry, I'm all **out** of 'em! I can't get **enough!** **Everybody** wants one!

Price gouging! Black Markets! Darn it! This gas shortage is making crooks out of everyone! Is there no decency left. . . ? !
Anything else you want?

Yes!
A siphoning hose!

. . . and I don't mind that you limited me to only eight gallons . . .
. . . but when you cut out giving GREEN STAMPS . . . that's going TOO FAR!!
GAS by APPOINTMENT ONLY
CAR WASH AND GAS. EITHER WAY WE CLEAN YOU OUT.

Hey, let's steal a car!

Look! This dude left his keys in the ignition! Like, man, he's askin' for it!
Jump in and let's take off!

Why isn't it starting?
No gas!
RRRR

Hey, let's steal a bike!

Aw, gee! There's **no gas** sold on **Sundays** any more!

That means we **can't visit** our **relatives** on **Sundays** any more!

And it means we **can't** go for long aimless **drives** in the **country** on **Sundays** any more!

This is **awful!** I don't know what I'm going to **DO** with myself on **Sundays** any more!
CLICK

Hey, remember when we were college kids back in the fifties, and we'd try to see how many of us we could stuff into one phone booth?!

Boy, were we stupid!
We weren't stupid! We were just young!

Oh, yeah? Well, NOW what's our excuse?!?
CAR POOL PICK UP POINT
87-VH
David Berg

THEN AND OWW! DEPT.

AND NOW,
FOR YOU NOSTALGIA FANS,
A LOOK BACK AT
THE OLD DAYS
WHEN THINGS WERE
A LOT DIFFERENT!

REMEMBER WHEN...

ARTIST: BOB CLARKE

WRITER: ARNIE KOGEN

REMEMBER WHEN...

... there were no fold-outs in magazines, and the biggest sex thrill was sneaking a look at "National Geographic" in your Dentist's waiting room!

REMEMBER WHEN...

... we used to suck lemons, not drive them!

REMEMBER WHEN...

... a "Pot Party" was a social gathering where women came to buy teflon fry pans!

REMEMBER WHEN...

... "Energy Crisis" meant you forgot to eat your *Wheaties!*

REMEMBER WHEN . . .

. . . George Washington's birthday was actually celebrated on George Washington's birthday!

REMEMBER WHEN . . .

. . . you not only didn't *watch* "Kung Fu"
. . . you weren't even allowed to *say* it!

REMEMBER WHEN . . .

. . . you slept on a "Water Bed"? No . . . not intentionally! You just woke up that way!

REMEMBER WHEN . . .

. . . girls wore long skirts? And how, if you wanted to know if a girl was knock-kneed, you had to listen!

REMEMBER WHEN . . .

. . . baseball teams used to trade players, not wives!

REMEMBER WHEN . . .

. . . Rest Rooms were simply marked "Men" and "Women"!

REMEMBER WHEN . . .

. . . we used to settle our problems over coffee and cigarettes? Now, *those* are our problems!

REMEMBER WHEN . . .

. . . a "bad trip" was an overnight train ride to visit your cousin in Schenectady!

DON MARTIN DEPT.

ONE MORNING

AT A BUS DEPOT

D. MARTIN..

COURT JESTING DEPT.

Tennis is one of the fastest-rising Sports in the country today. It seems that just about everybody is playing Tennis, and its rise in current popularity is amazing.

Well, we've decided to put an end to it once and for all... with

ARTIST: JACK DAVIS WRITER: LARRY SIEGEL

CHAPTER ONE

See the nice people.
They are playing Tennis.
See how civilized Tennis Players are.
See how they always compliment each other.
"Nice shot, Fred," one says.
How courteous they are.
"Sorry I missed that serve, Mike," another says.
What compassion they have.
"Good try. Mine was a lucky shot," says a third.
Soon they will leave the courts
And get in their cars
And curse each other
And run each other off the road
And steal each other's wives
And rob each other blind in business.
Tennis is a great sport
But it *does* interfere with the American Way of Life.

CHAPTER TWO

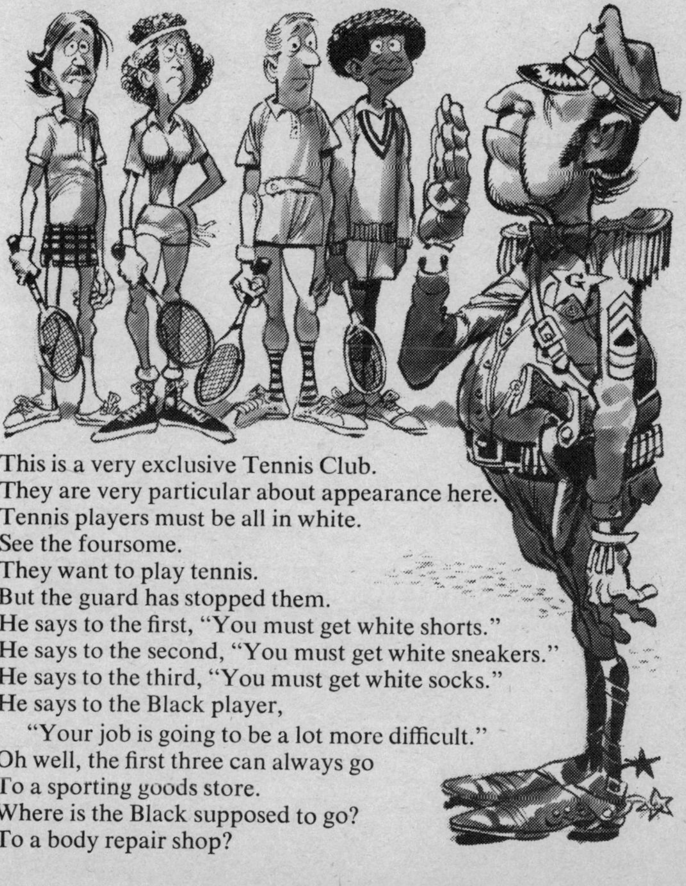

This is a very exclusive Tennis Club.
They are very particular about appearance here.
Tennis players must be all in white.
See the foursome.
They want to play tennis.
But the guard has stopped them.
He says to the first, "You must get white shorts."
He says to the second, "You must get white sneakers."
He says to the third, "You must get white socks."
He says to the Black player,
"Your job is going to be a lot more difficult."
Oh well, the first three can always go
To a sporting goods store.
Where is the Black supposed to go?
To a body repair shop?

CHAPTER THREE

See the doubles match.
Three men are playing with a girl.
The men are excellent players.
The girl is awful.
She leaps high for shots and misses.
She leans over for shots and misses.
She bends down for shots and misses.
She is not good.
She is not athletic.
She is not graceful.
Why do the men play with her?
She is not wearing a bra.

CHAPTER FOUR

Ha, ha, ha.
See the funny people.
See how their heads go from side to side to side
To side to side.
Wait a minute.
See the man in the middle.
His head is going up and down and up and down
And up and down.
What is going on here?
Very simple.
All the people are watching the Tennis game.
Except the man in the middle.
He is watching the girl
Without the bra.

CHAPTER FIVE

See the poor man.
He has been struggling on the court for two hours.
He is bathed in sweat.
He can hardly breathe.
He is exhausted.
His hand is bleeding.
But it was worth it.
He has won his battle.
Now that he has finally opened the vacuum-packed can of balls,
He is ready to play Tennis.

CHAPTER SIX

Who is this nice man?
He is called a Tennis Pro.
He teaches people how to play Tennis.
How does he teach them?
He gets 400 old balls
And tosses them over the net
And tells the people to hit them back.
After five minutes of this,
They spend 20 minutes helping him
Pick up the 400 balls.
Then they start over again.
For this the pro gets $30 an hour.
Now you know the true meaning of the term—
"Tennis Racket."

CHAPTER SEVEN

What is this man doing?
He is stringing a Tennis Racket.
Some Rackets are made of nylon.
This one is being made of gut.
The man is just about finished.
That didn't take very long.
It doesn't take much guts to make a racket.
The man will charge $75 for this one.
Now *that* takes guts.

CHAPTER EIGHT

There are many injuries peculiar to Tennis.
If you.don't serve with a full overhead motion
You can get "Tennis Elbow."
If you twist wrong on a backhand return
You can get "Tennis Shoulder."
What is this man doing?
He has just lost a match
And he is a true Tennis Gentleman,
So he is jumping 2½ feet over the net
To congratulate his opponent.
There is only one problem—
Tennis nets are 3 feet high.
Congratulations, idiot,
You just invented "Tennis Mouth."

CHAPTER NINE

What are these people doing?
They are waiting.
What are they waiting for? Lefty?
No.
Godot?
No.
The Robert E. Lee?
No.
They are waiting to get on a Public Tennis Court.
That can take a long, long time.
One of them is very angry.
He will write a letter of complaint to the City.
Or maybe the State.
No, he has decided to go clear to the top.
He's going to send a letter directly to Pres. Eisenhower.
Hmm, he's been waiting a lot longer than we thought.

CHAPTER TEN

See the Championship Tennis Player.
He has just won an important tournament.
See how the fans adore him.
He is very successful and very rich.
He has three cars, four homes,
And a yacht.
He makes over a half million a year.
Now that he has won this tournament
He will receive many lucrative Tennis offers,
But he will turn them all down.
Do you know why he will turn them down?
Because he doesn't want to turn Professional.
Isn't Amateur Tennis wonderful?
Some top performers make almost as much money
As College Football Players.

GRIN AND BEARER DEPT.

ON A

SAFARI

ARTIST & WRITER: ANTONIO PROHIAS

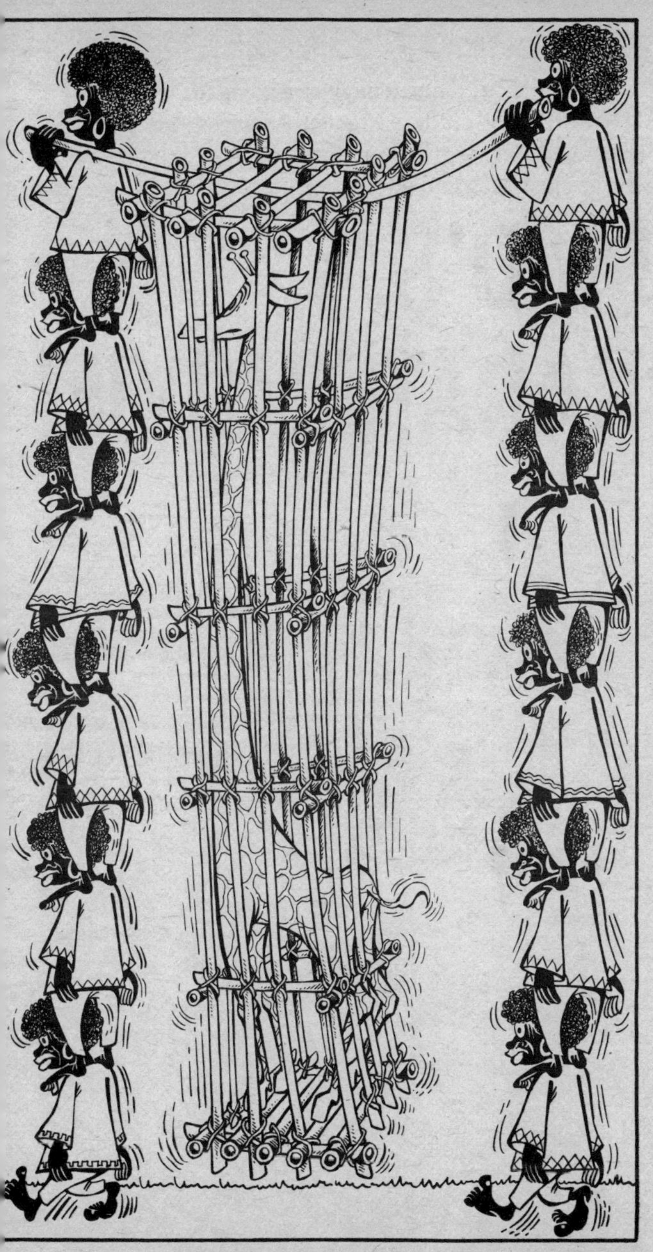

HACK FILM-MAKER DEPT.

Hello! I'm Mike Malice . . . and today we're going to do an "in depth" study of a recent Business Phenomenon! That's why I'm here with Mr. Kim Sai Shee, who has just been named

MAD'S "KARATE MOVIE"

ARTIST: JACK DAVIS   WRITER: STAN HART

PRODUCER OF THE YEAR

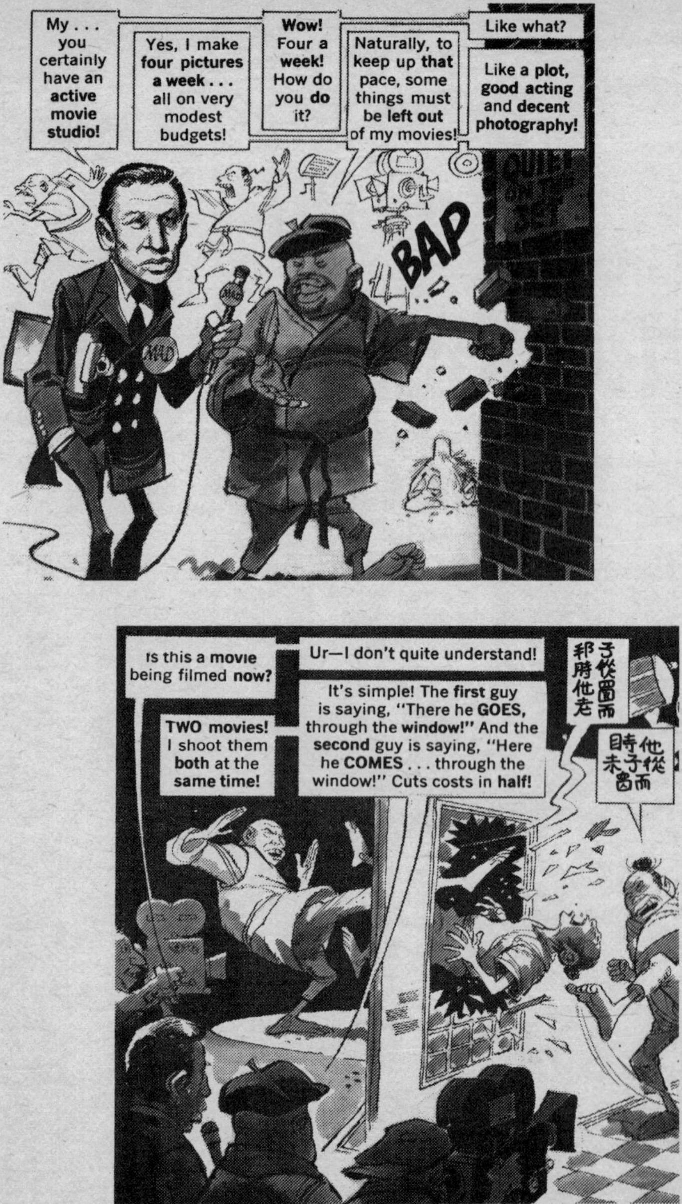

My . . . you certainly have an **active movie studio!**

Yes, I make **four pictures a week . . .** all on very modest budgets!

Wow! Four a **week!** How do you **do** it?

Naturally, to keep up **that** pace, some things must be **left out** of my movies!

Like what?

Like a **plot, good acting** and **decent photography!**

BAP

In every Karate movie, you need **two things!** One skinny **Hero,** and ten fat **Villains!** Here . . . the Villains are attacking the Hero, one at a time! They **always** attack the Hero, one at a time!
Is that an **old Chinese custom?**
No, silly!
Then **why** don't they **ALL** attack him at the **same time?**
If they **DID,** they'd beat his **brains** out!

Another feature of our movie is the **"Big Gang Battle"!** Fights with **two** or **three hundred people** are **not uncommon!**
My God! All those **actors!** It must cost you a **fortune!** How much do you **Day** each one?
Two pounds a day!
Two pounds? In English currency, that's . . .
What English currency! I'm talking about **RICE!**

Actors will work for only two pounds of rice?
Better still, they'll work for **nothing!** Watch this!
Attention, all Extras! I have only enough rice to pay **half** of you . . . so . . . **first come, first served!**
PAY MASTER

That's how I get my **mob fight scenes!** And for **half the price!**
Mr. Shee, I—I'm **shocked!** You are a **very unscrupulous person!**
Thanks, but **save** your **admiration** till our **next** stop!

Now . . . here is where we DUB IN the English dialogue! See the movie they are showing on the screen?
What about it?
Well, when we're through dubbing in THIS one, we cut it up, scene by scene, re-splice it, dub in ALL NEW dialogue and presto! We have TWO movies for the price of ONE!
But that's . . . dishonest!
Not at all! Actually, I'm only doing what the Critics tell people!
Oh . . . ? And what's that?
If you see ONE Karate Movie, you've seen them ALL!

Mr. Shoo, what are the most important elements in a Karate Movie?
Violence, gore, disfigurement and death! Mike, we show life like it really is!
But life isn't LIKE that!
It will be, after enough people start imitating what they see in my pictures!

What is your **biggest single expense** in making a Karate Movie?
Red paint! We use **buckets** of the stuff! Audiences just **love** the sight of **blood!** Unfortunately, we **ran out,** yesterday!
Did you **stop filming?**
Of course not! We merely made **a practical substitution!**
I know! You used **KETCHUP!**
No . . . **REAL KNIVES!!** Look . . . I just saved **four more pounds of rice!**

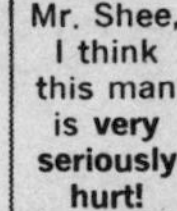

Mr. Shee, I think this man is **very seriously hurt!**
Nonsense! He only **LOOKS** very seriously hurt! Actually, he's **DEAD!**
And you feel no sense of **remorse?**
Life it **too short** for **regrets!** Look how short **HIS** was!

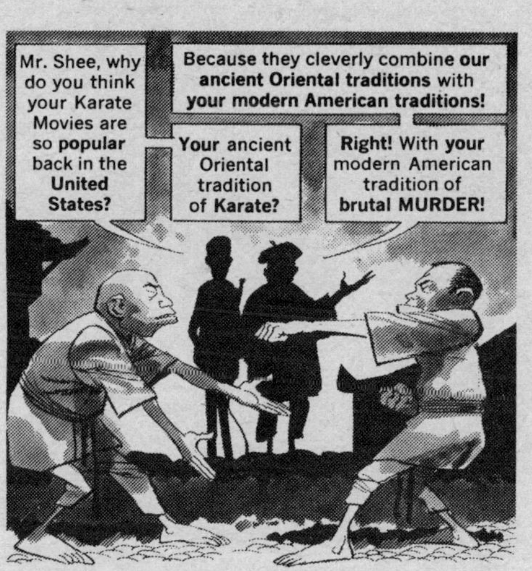
Mr. Shee, why do you think your Karate Movies are so **popular** back in the **United States?**
Because they cleverly combine **our ancient Oriental traditions** with **your modern American traditions!**
Your ancient Oriental tradition of **Karate?**
Right! With **your** modern American tradition of **brutal MURDER!**

They look **very good!**
The **ARE!** They have achieved the **second highest rank** that is **attainable** by Karate men! The **BLACK BELT!**
The **SECOND HIGHEST?** And what is the **FIRST** highest?
The belt that **I** have attained!
And what one is **that?**
The **MONEY BELT!** You will notice this interview isn't **all work** and **no fun!**

Here's an important scene from my **next** big Karate movie, **"Toes of Terror"**!

Why call it that?

Because the **Hero never bathes!**

See, the Villain's threatening to rip the Hero's **nose** off!

Yes, I see! Does he **do** it . . . ?

I sure **hope so!** I can't stand **happy endings!**

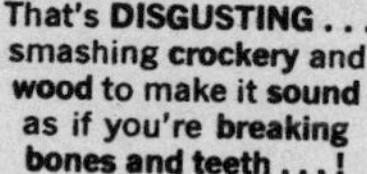
That's **DISGUSTING . . .** smashing **crockery** and **wood** to make it **sound** as if you're **breaking bones and teeth . . . !**

Don't be an **idiot!** We smash crockery and wood to **cover** the **REAL sound** of bones and teeth breaking!
That little girl is fighting for **Star Billing!** If she **lets up one little bit,** it's back to **"One from Column A, two from Column B . . ."** for her!
SNAP
CRASH
POP
KRACKLE
SNAP
SNAP
KACKLE
POP
SNAP
KLINK
TINKLE

Well, Mr. Shee . . . making a Karate Movie is certainly a **terrifying experience!**
Listen, I've got an even **MORE** terrifying experience for you . . .
NOW SHOWING

Sitting in the **audience . . . watching** a Karate Movie!
Man, I love **blood** and **gore** as much as the **next guy**, but a **Karate Movie Audience** is **SOMETHING ELSE!**
COMING SOON
KILL
KILL
KILL

KILL!
MAIM!
DISFIGURE!
HURT A LOT!
Well, they obviously enjoy encouraging the **Hero** of the movie!
What movie? They're encouraging a **little kid** in the **third row** who's arguing with his **Mother!**

This is the most revolting thing I've ever seen! How can you live with yourself . . . knowing that you promote immorality without a pang of conscience, while you brazenly cheat the American Public?!?
I feel a lot cleaner than the guy who produced the Documentary they're showing next!
What's that . . . ?
MAD

A SALUTE TO AMERICAN INDUSTRY
This is Mike Malice . . . turning you back to MAD Magazine . . .

WINDSHIELD WEEPERS DEPT.

With parking space at a minimum, and charges for parking at a maximum, the poor car owner has been trying various methods to beat the system while avoiding a ticket. Notes, official-looking identification cards. Police Department magazines, business cards, etc., are all being left in view in an

SURE-FIRE

attempt to convince the passing Cop to keep on passing. But they rarely work. Why? Because to really get to someone, you have to appeal to his emotions . . . to his feelings of guilt and insecurity. With this goal in mind, MAD herewith offers . . .

TICKET DETERRENTS FOR FRUSTRATED DRIVERS

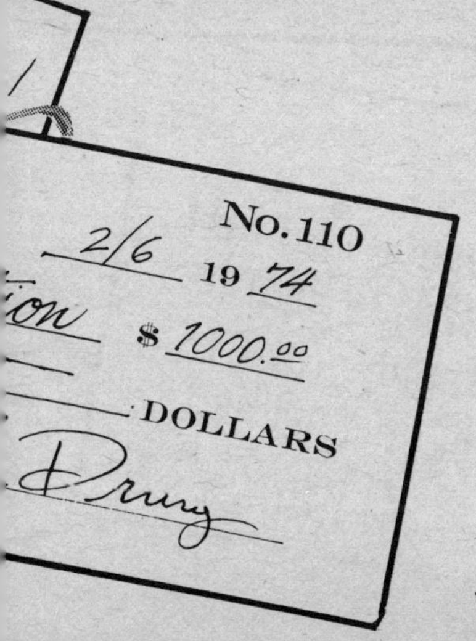

ARTIST: BOB CLARKE
WRITER: DICK DE BARTOLO

Mildred:
If you found my suicide note and traced me to the car, don't panic – I haven't done it yet.
I left the car here to go for a little walk to think about whether life is worth living. With all the setbacks I've had lately, all I need is one more bad experience to push me over the brink...

Dear Officer,
They just announced over the radio that this month's quota of parking tickets has already been reached.
Thanks!

This car is owned by a revered mother who just ran into the store to buy an American flag and an apple pie...

Bless, O Lord, the keeper of the Peace—the Officer of the Law— who in his own unselfishness, overlooks this minor trespass of another made in Your Image. But let he who rules with an iron hand—who puts him self before and above others— let him feel the pain of eternal damnation.

Amen!

MILTON ELNICK

CHIEF AUDITOR

INTERNAL REVENUE SERVICE

(Division of Tax Returns
Of City and State Employees)

*Officer—
Just went to pick
up my judicial robe.*

Madame Olga

THE WITCH WHO CAN PUT
THE CURSE ON ANYONE
...ANY TIME...ANYWHERE!
I NEVER FAIL!

CALL QZ-9-9977

I JUST RETURNED FROM VIET NAM AND I PUT THIS SIGN HERE FOR ALL TO SEE SO I COULD SAY HOW GREAT IT IS TO BE HOME IN A FREE COUNTRY WHERE YOU CAN GO WHERE YOU WANT, DO WHAT YOU WANT, *PARK* WHERE YOU WANT, AND NOT HAVE SOME COMMIE RAT HASSLE YOU! LONG LIVE THE AMERICAN WAY!

THIS CAR IS OWNED AND OPERATED BY THE:

CATHOLIC URBAN LEAGUE,

JEWISH NEIGHBORHOOD AID SOCIETY,

AND THE

PROTESTANT COMMUNITY ORGANIZATION

CAR POOL

Officer -

I heard on the radio that this make car has been recalled by the factory because a defective part may cause the steering wheel to fly off at any moment. So I immediately pulled over to the curb and left my car here not to take any chances.

DON MARTIN DEPT.

ONE FINE EVENING IN THE CASTLE

MMMMM....
SMACK

PAF

D.MARTIN..

HAM AND CHEERS DEPT.

A while back, Hollywood bestowed its coveted Academy Awards on various actors and actresses for outstanding performances in motion pictures. But all of us, in our daily lives, turn in many outstanding performances. And so . . . it seems only fair that we now present THE FIRST ANNUAL . . .

MAD ACADEMY AWARDS FOR BEST PERFORMANCES IN EVERYDAY SITUATIONS

ARTIST: PAUL COKER, JR.   WRITTEN BY: DICK DE BARTOLO & DON EPSTEIN

Ladies and Gentlemen, welcome to the **"The First Annual MAD Academy Awards For Everyday Situations"!** Here, in the garishly-decorated Grand Ballroom of the Hotel Garish, we have gathered to honor the people who have turned in the year's **"Best Performances"** when trapped in **"Everyday Situations"!** Er, we'll get on with the gala festivities in a moment! But first, will one of you **Stagehands** please adjust my **MIKE?**

Like to, Mac . . . but **Microphones** ain't in a **Scenery Mover's jurisdiction!** Er . . . maybe my **friend** over here could help you out . . .

I **could** adjust it for you as a **Prop Mover—normally!** But since it's **PLUGGED IN,** you have to get an **ENGINEER!!**

Sorry, fellas . . . but there's **no Award** this year for **"Passing The Buck"!** Maybe we'll add it to **NEXT** year's categories! Meanwhile, **on with the show . . .**

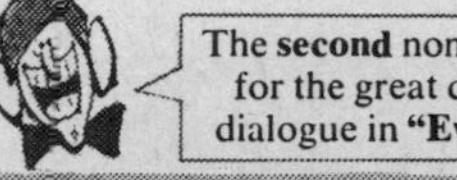

The **first** category is: **"BEST PERFORMANCE BY SOMEONE WHO'S GETTING A SPEEDING TICKET."** The **nominees** are: **Jack Hendle,** for the fabulous role he created in **"You're Right, But—"**...
I... I **know** I may have been going a **trifle fast,** Officer... but I was only trying to make it **home** before my **gas** ran out!
The **second** nominee is: **Jeannie Riptoff,** for the great delivery of her inspired dialogue in **"Everything's Relative"**...
After you write out my **ticket,** please give me your **name,** Officer! I want to tell my **Uncle Jake,** the **Chief of Police,** about the **swell job** you're doing!

The **third** nominee is **Malvina Mishigoss,** for her unforgettable version of **"December Bribe"** . . .

And the **Winner** is: **Roz Sheppard,** for her confusing but convincing performance in **"The New Math"** . . .

The **second** category is for **"BEST PERFORMANCE BY SOMEONE LEAVING A BORING PARTY."** The **first** nominee is **Al Muck** for **"Yawn With The Wind"** . . .

The **second** nominees are: **Kenneth** and **Sarah Badler,** who made such a great team in **"The Party's Overlong"** . . .

Sorry we have to **run,** folks . . . but we have to be home by **10 PM** because of our **pets!**

Oh? You have to walk your **dogs?**

No . . . our **goldfish** gets **lonely!**

The **third** nominees are: **Judy** and **Sid Plyth,** for their fine acting in **"Leave Story"** . . .

We hate to **run off** like this, gang, but tonight, of **all** nights, our **very favorite movie of all time** is on television. The **last** time we saw it, we were so **moved,** and it did so much to **enrich our lives** and gave us such a glimpse of **faraway places,** that we **swore** we'd **catch** the **re-run!**

You mean **"Dr. Zhivago"**?

No, **"Gidget Surfs To Rome"!**

And the **winner** is: **Stanley Sachs,** for his stellar job in **"What makes Stanny Run?"**. . .
Sorry I've got to leave the party so **early,** Bernice . . . but I must **rush right home** and start **packing** for my **trip!**
Oh? Where are you **going?**
To the **1976 Olympic Games!**

I do **love** these fun-filled **Award Ceremonies** with their witty acceptance speeches and their exciting surprise announcements . . . uh . . . but, unfortunately, I really must **rush right home** and start **packing** for my **trip!**
But you **already packed** for the **1976 Olympic Games!**
For the **1976** Olympic Games **yes!** But I don't want to wait until the **last minute** to pack for the **1980** Olympic Games!

The **next** category is **"BEST PERFORMANCE BY A KID WHO'S ALWAYS LATE FOR SCHOOL."** The **first** nominee is: **Scott Flink,** for his brilliant job in **"Don't Stop Me If You've Heard This"** . . .

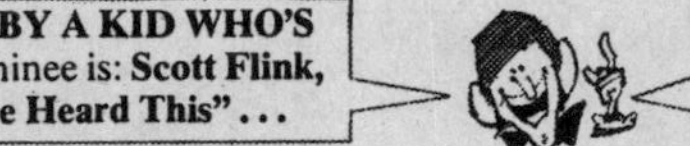

The **second** nominee is: **Phil Mintzer,** for his unanimously-acclaimed acting in **"After The Bull Is Over"** . . .

The **third** nominee is: **Tony Flinch,** for his excellent work in **"If You'll Buy This, You'll Buy Anything"** . . .
And the **winner** is: **Richard Shellis,** for his superb rendition of **"Dig That Dandy Lyin' "** . . .
Yesterday, you said you were tardy because you had to take care of your **old widowed Mother!** Is that your excuse **today, too?**
Oh, **no!** My Mother feels **fine!** Today, I had to take care of my **old widowed FATHER!**
cat
dog
epistemology
Sorry I'm **late** again, Miss Creatin, but after **milking the cows, feeding the chickens** and **slopping the pigs,** I had to walk down **twelve flights of stairs** because the **elevator** in my **apartment house** wasn't working this morning!

Mr. Shellis couldn't **make** it, so **I'm** here to accept his Award! He told me to tell you he's **stuck** in his **TRACTOR!**
Somewhere out in a **field?**
No . . . somewhere between his **Living Room** . . . and his **Bedroom!**
The **next** category is: **"BEST PERFORMANCE BY A GIRL WHO WASN'T INVITED TO A PROM."** The **first** nominee is: **Ursula Urpman,** for her memorable **"Who Needs It?" . . .**
If one had nothing **better** to do, I suppose that going to a **silly Prom** would be a **good way** to **kill a few hours!** But I'm afraid it's rather **far down** on my list of **really fantastic things to do!**
Gee, you're lucky! Uh— fantastic things like **what . . . ?**
Well . . . I have to return some **books** to the Library . . . and then I have to file my **nails** . . . and then I have to **clean up my room** . . . and then I have to . . .

The **second** nominee is: **Tanya Blish,** who tugged at our heartstrings in **"Alone Again, Naturally" . . .**

The **third** nominee is: **Penelope McNee,** whose inspired performance was so magnificent in **"Fibber McNee" . . .**

The third nominees are: Martin Gale and Jodi Bogg, for their marvelous job in "Two For The Show" . . .
W-we found out they're showing a film in our next class . . .
. . . and we wanted to get our eyes accustomed to the dark!
And the Winners are: Arnold Bunglewald and Cindy Meister for their fantastic "Learn By Doing" . . .
We were doing our HOMEWORK, Miss Markowitz!
What kind of HOMEWORK can you do in a CLOSET??
Our "SEX EDUCATION" Homework!!

Thanks so much for this fabulous Award! We're going to take it into the closet at school, and watch it glow in the dark!
But it doesn't glow in the dark!
WE know that, and YOU know that . . . but MISS MARKOWITZ doesn't know that! It's our next excuse when she catches us in the closet again!
And that's our "MAD Academy Awards For Best Performances In Everyday Situations"! But starting right now, we'll be looking for contenders for next year's Awards! So—who knows?!? Maybe you'll find yourself as a nominee in next year's five fun-filled pages!
But before we go, we'd like to present a Special Award to our Emcee for his truly great performance in our "Boy . . . Am I Putting You On" category . . . for going through this year's five pages of dribble as if they really had some humorous social significance!

And the **Winner** is: **Susan Calabash,** for putting her heart and soul into **"Who's Kidding Who?"** . . .

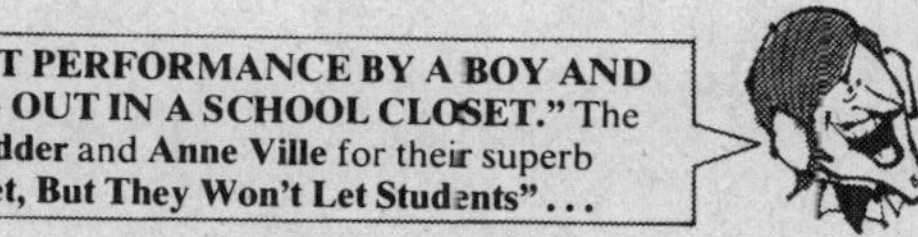

And the **last** category is **"BEST PERFORMANCE BY A BOY AND GIRL CAUGHT MAKING OUT IN A SCHOOL CLOSET."** The **first** nominees are **Josh Kidder** and **Anne Ville** for their superb teamwork in **"Teachers Pet, But They Won't Let Students" . . .**
And the **second** nominees are: **Ronnie Furshlugginer** and **Heidi Swisschick,** for their outstanding rendition of **"Please Don't Tell Our Parents" . . .**

And just **what** are you two **doing** in there?
We . . . *uh* . . . we're working on a **"Career Guidance Project,"** Miss Glumm! I was helping Anne **train** for her future profession as a **Hat-Check Girl!**

Ronnie and Heidi! Come out of that closet **this instant!!**
But, **Miss Galvin . . .** you **KNOW** that the **Supreme Court** has **outlawed prayers** in the **Classroom . . .**
. . . so **we were** doing our **praying** in **HERE!!**

BUMPER STICKERS DEPT.

There are more conservation groups and ecology clubs in America than ever before. Unfortunately, there are also more cars on the road than ever before, and it isn't hard to guess who's winning the daily battle between automobile and animal. With this in mind, we now propose a more practical handbook for nature study—one geared to help the reader identify Mother Nature's creatures as we most often view them . . .

ARTIST & WRITER: AL JAFFEE IDEA BY: ROBERT KAUFMAN

Chapter I IDENTIFYING WILDLIFE

One of the great pleasures of driving is identifying the specimens one comes across in one's travels, not to mention specimens that other motorists have run across in *their* travels. Perhaps the most convenient way is when you've returned home, you can leisurely study and identify the specimens indelibly etched on your car.

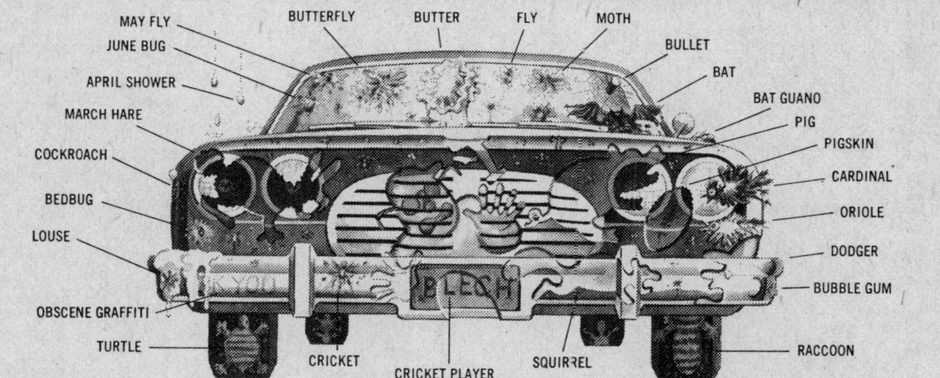

The key to specimen identification is to learn what nature's creatures look like in their *altered state*. It is important not to confuse wildlife with other things, such as the windblown refuse thrown out of the windows of other cars. Then too, the splotch from a praying mantis could easily be confused with the splotch from a preying pigeon with accurate aim. A few weeks of hard study is all anyone ever needs to become expert, so stick with it!

Chapter III

IDENTIFYING WILDLIFE BY SOUND

Most highway specimens are created at night. But, of course, in the dark viewing is sometimes impossible. The *serious* highway wildlife collector must learn the *sounds* of his prey. The following examples will start you off on the right road! Allow for minor differences in specimen sounds depending upon locale.

THE SOUND YOU HEARD

WHUMP!

WHAT CAUSED IT

THE SOUND YOU HEARD

WHUMP! WHUMP!

WHAT CAUSED IT

THE SOUND YOU HEARD
WHUMP! WHUMP! THWAMP!
WHAT CAUSED IT
THE SOUND YOU HEARD
THUP! THUP! THUP! THUP! THUP! THUP!
WHAT CAUSED IT
TURTLE CROSSING
THE SOUND YOU HEARD
WHUMP! WHUMP! THWAMP! BADAM!
WHAT CAUSED IT
THE SOUND YOU HEARD
SQUISH-SH-SH-SH-SH-SH-SH-SH
WHAT CAUSED IT

Chapter VI
CONSERVATION

With conservation uppermost in our minds today, we must think of those that follow us on life's broad highway. We must not selfishly enjoy, but learn to share. With this in mind, *Motorist's Guide* recommends all wildlife enthusiasts utilize the shatter-proof, low silhouette plastic covers available in a variety of shapes and sizes and which are easily stored in your rear trunk.

To conserve your specimen so others can delight in your findings also, merely place appropriate sized cover over it. Its self-sticking adhesive edge will keep everything in place for weeks.

Chapter IX

ROAD HAZARDS FOR ENTHUSIASTS

Due to the scanning nature of the wildlife enthusiast's driving style, he often devotes too little time to familiar road signs and responds reflexively to their warnings.

A case in point is when a driver observes the typical "curve in the road" caution and turns the wheel automatically . . .

. . . only to find the "warning" was nothing more than a snake flung across a blank billboard by a previous car!

Chapter XII PHOTOGRAPHS AND TROPHIES

A hit is as good as a miss if you end up with nothing to show for it. Two popular ways of showing off specimens that you may personally encounter are photos and mounted trophies. Here are some helpful tips on both methods.

PHOTOGRAPHS

Always plan your shot around the features that will best identify your specimen, assuming, of course, some identifiable characteristics remain. Consider the examples of *good* and *bad* shots that follow.

GOOD SHOT Overhead view of turtle

BAD SHOT Side view of turtle

TROPHIES

Mounting trophies is strictly a matter of personal taste, and thus little can be said about it. One hint, however, is that you carry a hacksaw in your trunk for cutting road signs "that tell a story." These will invariably prove to be the best souvenirs of your trip!

Chapter XV CHARTING SPECIMENS

Like any great sport, a 'score card' is half the fun. A specimen chart for charting specimens that any wildlife enthusiast will find simple to make and pleasurable to use follows below:

My trip across Northwest U.S.A. from July 20, 1973 ending August 6, 1973

SPECIMENS SIGHTED BY ME	SPECIMENS STRUCK BY ME	SPECIMENS STRUCK BY OTHERS	SPECIMENS OFF THE ROAD	SPECIMENS ON THE ROAD	SPECIMENS STILL BOUNCING AROUND	GENERAL CONDITION OF SPECIMENS
24 rabbits	8	16	5	9	10	Disgusting
8 Bears	3	5	5	2	1	Fair
14 Racoons	11	3	2	11	1	Good
9 Snakes	3	6	3	2	4	Yecch!
27 Squirrels	12	15	8	16	3	Pleasant
4 moose	1	3	2	1	1	Very Good
2 Elk	2	0	1	1	0	Aromatic
1 llama	1	0	0	0	1	So-So
10,031 insects	10,027	4	0	4	0	REVOLTING the rest were on the car

JOKE AND DAGGER DEPT.

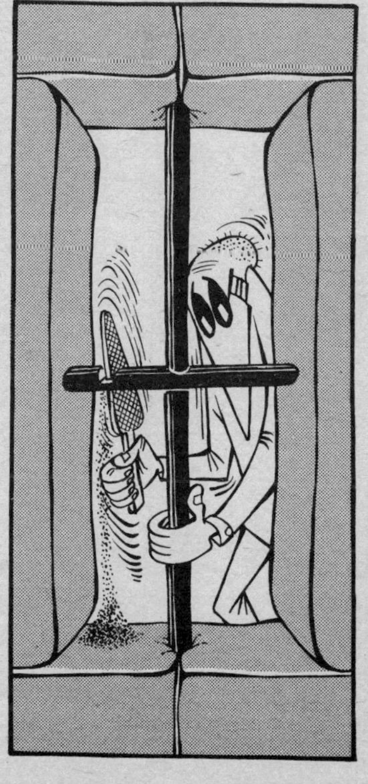

Prohías

THE OLD CRYSTAL BALLGAME DEPT.

MAD'S Sure-Fire SPORTS PRED

For The Upcoming Season

ARTIST: JACK DAVIS WRITER: PAUL PETER PORGES

ICTIONS

A sports idol of the nation's youth will be arrested for speeding, indecent exposure and possession of marijuana.

A violent fight will break out as both benches rush onto the field, but the TV camermen will only pan waving fans.

Trailing by 1 point with 12 seconds left, the Home Team will steal the ball, drive downcourt and set up their top scorer... when the telecast will lose the video portion.

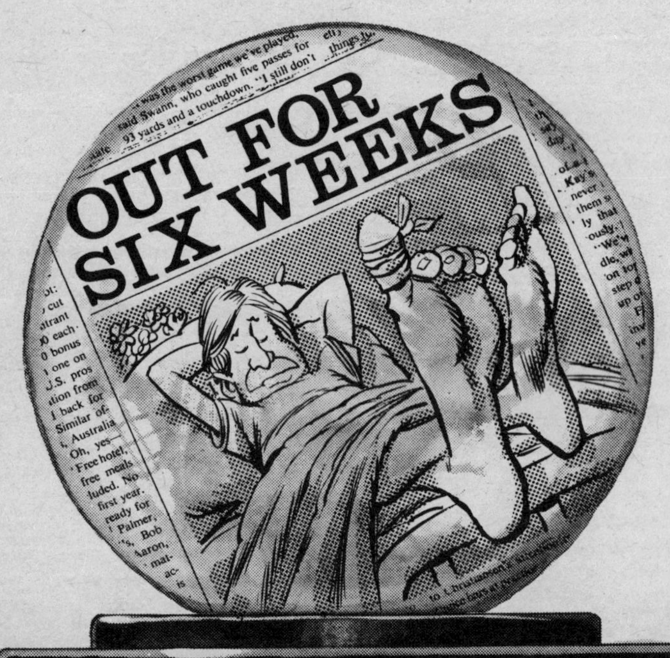

The Superstar of your favorite team... upon whom all hope for any chance at winning the title depends... will be injured and knocked out of play for the rest of the season.

A first round draft choice Consensus All-American, no-cut contract Bonus Rookie will not live up to expectations.

You will watch 25 minutes of rain pelting a wet tarpaulin before a big game will be called because of bad weather.

An All-Pro Star will disappear from training camp, and re-appear in a Southern California mystic health commune. He'll then put down Football on the Johnny Carson Show.

At mid-season, the leading team will make the cover of a big national magazine...and then proceed to lose nearly 80% of their remaining games, winding up in third place.

MINOR ADJUSTMENT DEPT.

In past issues, we've taken "A MAD Look At Two College Generations" and "A MAD Look At Two High School Generations." With *this* article, we continue our pattern of regression . . . as we compare the *pre-adolescent* of the 40's with the younger set of today in this last (we hope) of a series entitled:

A MAD LOOK AT TWO GRAMMAR SCHOOL GENERATIONS

ARTIST: PAUL COKER, JR.

WRITER: LOU SILVERSTONE

DISCIPLINE . . . THEN . . .

. . . AND NOW . . .

READING MATERIAL... THEN...

...AND NOW...

MOVIES . . . THEN . . .

. . . AND NOW . . .

HEROES... THEN...

...AND NOW...

BICYCLES ... THEN ...

... AND NOW ...

RACE RELATIONS... THEN...

...AND NOW...

EDUCATION IN THE HOME... THEN...

...AND NOW...

SCHOOL TEACHERS . . . THEN . . .

. . . AND NOW . . .

POLITICS . . . THEN . . .

. . . AND NOW . . .

SPORTS... THEN...

...AND NOW...

DON MARTIN DEPT.

AT "THE NATIONAL ASSOCIATION OF PROFESSIONAL GLASS-EATERS" BANQUET

COKE

KRUNCHLE
KRAKLE
SHKLINK
SKROTCH

CHONK
KRAKLE
GLUK

TOOF THAFF
FAK

D. MARTIN....

See, here, Waiter!! There's a FLY in my parfait glass! What are you trying to do . . . make me sick??

BERG'S-EYE VIEW DEPT.

THE LIGHTER SIDE OF...

THE

ARTIST & WRITER:
DAVE BERG

HOLIDAY SEASON

Boy, am I glad to be getting away from this hell-hole of a school for the Holidays!
Where are you going?
Back home!

When I get there, I'll give my folks the "Big Hello" . . .
And then they'll give me the "Big Put-Down" about my long hair and my pot smoking and my shocking attitudes toward money, sex and all that jazz!

Then, I'll bug them about their dumb Middle Class morality! And they'll scream at me! And I'll scream at them! And then I'll blow, and hang around the local gin mill or watch TV in my room, and I'll do a lot of counting!
Counting what . . . ?!?

Counting the days till I can get back here to this lovely hell-hole of a school!

This is the **prettiest season** of the year! Everything is so **attractively decorated** and **beautifully illuminated!** This block of yours is **particularly** stunning! Each house is lit up **more spectacularly** than the **next!** You must be **very proud!**
NOEL
SEASONS GREETINGS

I **used to be** . . . when I was the **only** one on the block who **did** it! Then, those **dirty rat-fink neighbors** of mine all began to **copy** me! The **lousy so-and-so's** poured fortunes of **money** into their decorations, trying to **out-do** me . . . and **show me up!**

Why, those bums have overdone it **so much,** they've **completely minimized** the effect of **MY decorations** and **message** . . .
PEACE ON EARTH GOOD WILL TOWARD MEN

And how was YOUR joyous Christmas morning, Sonny?
It wasn't so joyous!

The whole family was there . . . Gran'ma, Gran'pa, Mom an' Dad, Aunts, Uncles, Cousins, Sisters an' Brothers! And there was such hollarin' and carryin' on!
"It's not fair! You gave her a better present than you gave me!"
"His costs more than mine costs!"
. . . and awful stuff like that!

Well, that's to be expected when it comes to Children! It's called Sibling Rivalry!

Yeah, but it wasn't the Children doing the hollaring! It was the GROWN-UPS!!

MERRY CHRISTMAS, EVERYBODY!!

What do you mean, "Merry Christmas, Everybody!!"? Do you realize that for people who live alone, Christmas can be the saddest time of the year?
I—I never thought of it that way! And YOU live alone, so you're one of those people, aren't you?

Sa-a-ay! You're spending the Holidays with US!! Gee, Christmas must've been HELL for you all these years, huh, Sid?

Not since I started using this sob story, it hasn't!

Ooohh! Am I sick! My head is exploding! I'm making a New Year's resolution!! I will never . . . NEVER do what I did THIS New Year's again . . . EVER!!!

Boy, you look terrible! You must've really tied one on!
Sorry, but I don't drink!

Aw, c'mon! Don't kid me! It's obvious that you're suffering from too many trips to the Punch Bowl!
The Punch Bowl? No, I missed that one!

But I must've seen every other one they televised . . . the Sugar Bowl, the Orange Bowl, the Cotton Bowl, the Gator Bowl, the Tangerine Bowl, the Sun Bowl . . . Ooooh! Am I sick!

You hang your stocking up there on the fireplace . . . and Santa Claus will come down the chimney and fill it with toys and goodies!

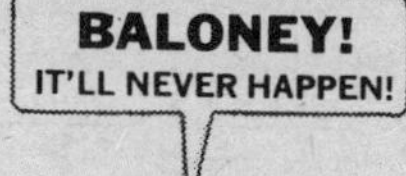
BALONEY!
IT'LL NEVER HAPPEN!

Don't you believe in Santa Claus?
Sure I do!

But I DON'T believe in phony fireplaces that haven't got any chimneys!

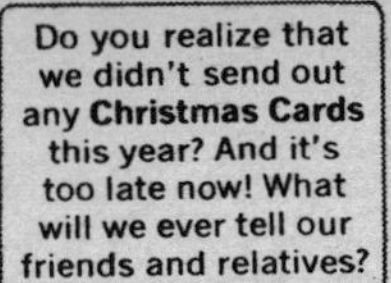
Do you realize that we didn't send out any **Christmas Cards** this year? And it's too late now! What will we ever tell our friends and relatives?

Tell 'em we broke our writing hands, **skiing!**
No . . . they'll **never** believe **that** story!
Tell 'em we both came down with the **Flu,** and couldn't bring ourselves to lick the **stamps** and spread the **disease!**

No . . . they'll **never** believe **that!**
Tell 'em we **sent out** the cards . . . but the lousy new **Postal System** LOST them!

THAT THEY'LL BELIEVE!

Gee, this is a very expensive Christmas present you're buying for your Dad!
Why not? He's a great guy, and he deserves the best!

There's no Generation Gap in OUR family! My Dad is fantastic with the kids! He digs the whole scene! He works like a dog, and he's a great provider!

Er . . . how do you plan to pay for this?
With my Dad's Charge Plate!

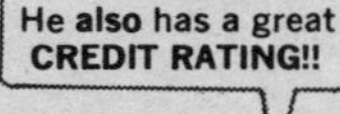
He also has a great CREDIT RATING!!

H-h-hello, Mom?? I—I thought I'd call you up and wish you a Happy New Year!
The same to you! What's the matter? I can hear it in your voice! You can't fool a Mother's heart! Something's wrong!

Nothing's wrong, Mom! It's just a bummer to be alone on New Year's Eve!
You poor thing! Where are you?

In a phone booth . . . on Times Square . . .
STATE
SEX
PORNO
HAPPY NEW YEAR!

I want a plastic model toy of the M-16 Rifle, a model kit of an "Honest John" Rocket Launcher, and a model of a B-52 Bomber!

I also want a Size 10 complete Football Uniform with shoulder pads and helmet and shoes and the whole bit, plus a complete Baseball Uniform with glove!

I'm sure your son will enjoy all these Christmas presents!
SON?! I'll have you know these things are all for my ten-year-old DAUGHTER!!

Haven't you ever heard of WOMEN'S LIB . . . ?!?

One Round-Trip Ticket to New York's **Kennedy Airport,** please!
Sorry! All flights are **booked solid!**
Merry Christmas

You gotta be **kidding!**
No, I'm **not!** Most reservations over Christmas are made **months in advance!**

But I'm—I'm **desperate!** I just **GOTTA** get home for the **Holidays!**
Oh, well, in **THAT** case, we can **help** you!

We **still** have some space available over **EASTER!!**

Boy, when it comes to the **Holiday Season,** everybody has their **hands** out . . . saying, **"Gi'me! Gi'me!"**
I know! I know!
WILLIAM M. GAINES

I had to tip the **Janitor,** the **Doormen,** the **Postmen,** the **Garbagemen** . . . and a lot of **other** moochers!
I know! I know!

It's nothing but a form of **LEGALIZED RIP-OFF!**
I know! I know! I've got the **same troubles!**
David Berg

Here's your **Christmas Bonus!**

DON MARTIN DEPT.

ONE FINE DAY

DURING THE CIVIL WAR

THWOP

RIP

ZWEET

D. MARTIN...

WISE GUIDE DEPT.

MAD has come up with a device to shake up those indifferent and incompetent people you too often find yourselves at the mercy of. It's called a "Rattler". A Rattler is not something you use on the Innocent, but rather as a Defensive Weapon on people who intimidate you: the surly cab driver, the wise-guy waiter, the nasty sales clerk . . . anyone who has developed an inverted snobbery about his work and views anyone less expert as an inferior. If you run into such a person, why not try out some of these . . .

ARTIST: JACK DAVIS WRITER: LARRY GORE

...FOR SHAKING UP **WAITERS AND WAITRESSES**

No . . . I'd only like **HALF** a table! I'm not very **hungry!**

I'd like an **empty plate!** I'm on a **very strict diet!**

How about sitting down and **joining** me? Then we can **split the check,** and I won't have to leave a **tip!**

Can you bring me some **extra silverware!** I have the **same set** at home, and **I'm missing** a few pieces!

I'll have the **same** thing that I ordered yesterday! I **didn't TOUCH it** yesterday!

I'll have the **steak dinner** . . . with no potatoes . . . no vegetables . . . and no **meat!**

The **menu** looks **good!** I'll eat **THAT!**

I'm very **intimidated** by **Waiters!** So may I **start tipping** you **NOW?**

Miss, would you be **offended** if I **sent out** for some **food?**

My compliments to the **Chef** . . . for having the **nerve** to pass **this stuff** off as **food!**

Hey, this food isn't **half bad** . . . it's **ALL bad!**

Waiter, give me a **very small check!** I'm in a **hurry!**

. . . FOR SHAKING UP **BARBERS**

I know it's my turn, but I just can't stop reading these **three-year-old magazines!**

Before you touch my hair, can you show me **proof** that you're **Italian?**

I'd like it **longer** in the **back,** . . . and **thicker** on **top,** please!

Never mind the **haircut!** Just tell me your idiotic **opinions!**

Tell me, do you **shave legs?**

...FOR SHAKING UP **CAB DRIVERS**

...FOR SHAKING UP **SALES HELP**

...FOR SHAKING UP **ELEVATOR OPERATORS**

To the **Penthouse,** driver . . . and **don't stop** for any **lights!**

Do you get **extra pay** for flying **dangerous missions?**

How could they send a **kid** up in a crate like **this?**

Twice around the **building,** driver! We're in **love!**

Would the **4th floor** take you out of your way?

Here's a buck! Take me to **another building!**

Uh . . . where's the **Men's Room** in this car? I think I'm going to be **sick . . .**

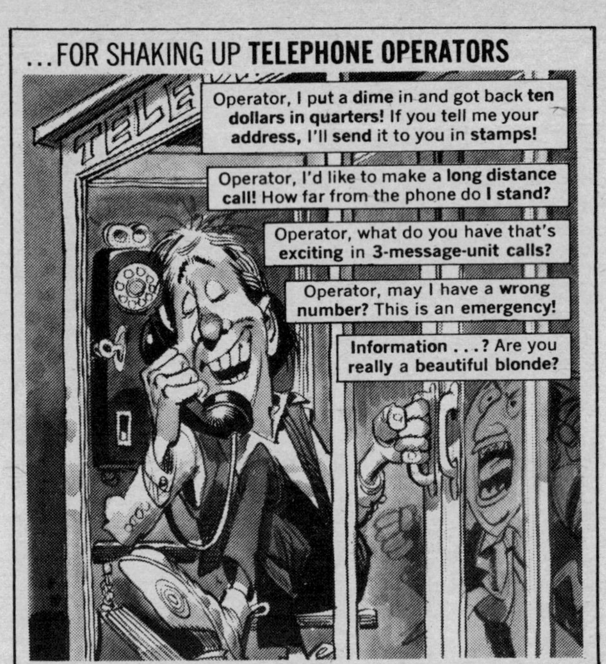
...FOR SHAKING UP TELEPHONE OPERATORS
TELE
Operator, I put a dime in and got back ten dollars in quarters! If you tell me your address, I'll send it to you in stamps!
Operator, I'd like to make a long distance call! How far from the phone do I stand?
Operator, what do you have that's exciting in 3-message-unit calls?
Operator, may I have a wrong number? This is an emergency!
Information . . . ? Are you really a beautiful blonde?

PLAINSCLOTHESMAN DEPT.

Would a hard-riding, gun-toting, square-jawed, straight-shooting Marshal from New Mexico really help New York solve its crime problem? We think it's an idiotic idea . . . even for Television! But that's what they're actually trying to sell us with . . .

ARTIST: ANGELO TORRES
WRITER: LOU SILVERSTONE

Good **afternoon,** McClod! I'm glad you're just **visiting** us! I don't know about **New Mexico,** but here in **New York,** gangsters get up **bright** and **early,** and we expect our **Police Officers** to **at least** do the **same!**
Now, Chief! Don' get all heated up! It was so **nice,** Ah decided to walk through **Central Park!**
McClod, **nobody**—especially a **Cop**—walks through Central Park!
Ah know! But Ah like t' mosey along the **Bridle Path!** Reminds me of **home!** Anyway, Ah **stumbled on t' somethin'!**
So I **noticed!** Next time you decide to walk along a Bridle Path, take off your **BOOTS** before you come in here!
A'm tryin' **t' tell** yuh! Ah discovered a gang of **RUSTLERS** in Central Park!
Listen, McClod! We've got **con men, muggers, rapists, murderers** . . . we've even got **Shakespeare in the Park!** The one thing we **DON'T** have is **Rustlers** . . . mainly because there's **nothing** to **rustle!!**
Shor there is! **BY-CYCLES!**

Yessir, Ah saw a couple of fellers **rustlin'** **bikes!**
Allegedly, McClod, you are a **Police Officer!** That means that if you witness a **Felony,** you are supposed to **ARREST** the perpetrators!
Ah know that, Chief! But Ah figure **Bike Rustlin's** a whole lot like **Cattle Rustlin'!** And it don't make much **horse sense** to arrest the **Hired Hands!** You gotta go after the **HEAD HONCHO!**
POLICE
So Ah'd like **t' join up** with that gang, find out who the **Boss** is . . . and **THEN** we corral 'em!
How do you plan on doing **that,** McClod! Are you going to look up **"Bike Rustlers"** in the **Yellow Pages?**
That wouldn't do me much good! Ah still get throwed by them new-fangled **dial phones!** Now, back in **Tacos,** all we gotta do is lift the receiver and tell the **Operator** what number we want! In fact, there's this **ONE** Operator named **Amy Lou—**

McClod, I don't CARE about Amy Lou! How do you plan on infiltrating the gang?
Simple! Ah'll jus' go into th' Bike Rustlin' business mahself, and then the gang will invite me to join 'em!
That sounds dangerous, Simp! You could get KILLED!
You mean "killed" like in DEAD?!?
Hmmm! That part is really tempting! But . . . I'm afraid I already have a special assignment for you, McClod!
There yuh go, Chief!
Dawgone! Ah don' mind bein' assigned to the Meter Maids

. . . but Ah shore wish Ah didn't have t' wear the Official UNIFORM!
Chief, they just found McClod unconscious!
How could they TELL?
McClod! What happened to you? Did a Parking Meter fall on you?
No, Chief! I figured I'd work on the By-cycle Case in my spare time, so I swiped a bike! But the training wheels fell off!

I told you to stay away from that Bike Caper, McClod . . .
Ah'd like to hang around and shoot the breeze awhile, but Ah got me some bikes to rustle!
McClod!!
Forget it! He's gone!
KEEP OFF
Hel-l-l-lp!! Police! That Texas Transvestite just stole my little boy's bike!
And now, Ladie-e-es and Gentlemen, the Great Spumoni and his death-defying high wire bicycle ride . . .
Stoppa that man! He's-a steal-a my bicycletto!!

Simp McClod! What are you doing in this place?
Oh, howdy, Crass! Ah was jest tryin' t' steal this by-cycle, but no matter how hard I pedal the durned thang, it won't budge an inch!
Why haven't you returned my calls, McClod?
Ah been busier'n a one-armed farmhand at milkin' time!
McClod, is there someone else?
No way! Yore purty, educated, sophisticated an' rich! We got a lot in common!
Cowboy . . . we're ALL pretty, educated, sophisticated, rich . . . AND available!
Lay off! He's mine!
And we dig the rugged, outdoor homespun type!
No—he's mine!
Wal, Ah'll say one thang fer Big City gals! They ain't got much meat on their bones, but Ah shor do admire their taste in men!

Glad you could get here, Chief! I got some bad news for you! McClod—
You're right! He IS bad news! So don't talk about him! Let me enjoy this bank robbery!
That's just it, Chief! McClod's inside the bank!
Inside the BANK?!? I thought he was stealing bicycles! What'd he do, decide to branch out?!?
BANK
McClod's made so much bread stealing bikes, he had to open a bank account! He's one of the hostages!
NOW HEAR THIS IN THERE! LET THE HOSTAGES GO! ALL EXCEPT McCLOD! HIM—YOU CAN KEEP!
Nobody's coming out, Chief . . .
Okay! Let's rush 'em!!

POLICE OFFICERS!! NOBODY MOVE!!
McClod, what happened to the bank robbers?!?
Y--you let them get away with the money?
That makes TWO of us McClod! I don't want anybody to know you're a Cop, either!
There yuh go, Chief!
They went out the skylight!
Ah'm supposed to be a bike thief, Chief! Ah don' want anybody t' know Ah'm a Cop!

McClod, you are to stay off this Bike Case—even during your lunch hours! Since you've been on it, bike stealing has reached epidemic proportions! Would you believe somebody even stole the MAYOR's bike?!
Ah know! It's a ten-speeder! Ah jest may keep that one fer mahself!
I'm taking over the Bike Case personally! Go home, put your skirt on and report back to the Meter Maids!

Get in the car, Man! We're gonna take you for a little ride!
There yuh go! No matter what they say about you Big City folks, yo're the friendliest people I have EVER met!!
So you're the character who's been stealing bikes in our territory! Thanks to you, we've been having trouble meeting our quota!
And if we're in trouble . . . so are YOU!
Wal, Ah'll be glad to share yor trouble, fellers! Back home, we always say, "The burden seems a whole lot lighter when a few Jackasses share the load!" . . .

This is the **end** of the **trail** for you, Cowboy!
Hey, Ah got a much **better** idee! How about me **joinin' up** with yor gang?
How do we know you're not a **Cop?**
Accordin' t' the **Police Manual,** it says, "No duly authorized Officer of the Law shall wear a **mustache!"** An' this ain't no **cactus** a-growin' on my upper lip!

Hey, you seem to know a **lot about Police Regulations!**
Ah watch a lot of **TV!**
Sounds reasonable! Okay, Cowboy— you're **in!**
There yuh go! Now, when do Ah get to meet the **Head Honcho?**

No one gets to meet "Mr. Big"! We get our orders over the phone! And let me warn you, Cowboy! Any funny business, and they're gonna find you floating in that river!
Don' worry, Pardner! Ah'd rather be DAID than float in THAT river!
Chief, will you accept a Collect Call from McClod?
What's the matter, McClod! Don't you have a dime?
How yuh doin', Chief!? It's a funny thang, but the phone booths here don't take dimes!
Don't be stupid! All phone booths take dimes!
Not in Hong Kong they don'!!
N.Y.P.D.

McClod!! What are you doing in HONG KONG?!?
Why, Ah'm talkin' t' YOU on the phone, Chief!
You could have done that in New York! Why there?!?
Ah've infiltrated the bike gang, Chief! We steal bikes in New York, ship 'em here, paint 'em, and ship 'em back to New York!
Why would anyone want to ship stolen bikes 7000 miles just to paint them!?
Probably 'cause the Labor is a lot cheaper here! They gotta take 'em apart, paint 'em, fill 'em up—
FILL THEM UP?!? With WHAT . . . ?!?
That funny li'l white powder . . .
HEROIN!! McClod, you've stumbled onto The Hong Kong Connection!

Hang up the phone, Cowboy!
McClod?!? Are you there? Mc—CLICK! 
Well, you had me fooled, Hayseed! I figured you were too stupid to be a Cop! Shows you how bad things are these days! You know, of course, that now I have to kill you!
Hey, not yet! Ain't it Standard Procedure fer a TV Crook t' explain the entire operation t' the TV Cop jest b'fore he rubs 'im out?
You already KNOW how we operate!
Everythin' 'cept one detail! Who's runnin' th' show?
You're looking at him, Cowboy! I'm the legendary "Mr. Big"!

Don' try t' hog-tie me! Yo're jest one of the Hired Hands!
That's what I wanted everyone to think! If the Police suspected that I was only a petty Bicycle Thief, they'd never bother me! They'd be more interested in nailing "Mr. Big"! Now to get rid of you! Say your prayers . . .
Hold on! Y-Yo're not gonna SHOOT me, are yuh?
No, this isn't a gun! This is a cigarette lighter, and I'm offering you a light!
Wait a cotton-pickin' minute! Wouldn't it make a lot more sense if'n my death looked like an accident?!?
You're right! An accident would be much neater!
Gulp!! Maybe Ah'd be better off if'n Ah'd jest let him shoot me!

Wal, at least Ah'll die with mah boots on, even if th' "stampede" is only a fork-lift truck!
If only Ah had a stretch of rope t' make a lassoo!
Hey! There yuh go!
GOTCHA! 
We're from the Hong Kong Police! Nobody move!
YAAAIIIIIIIIIIIIIII!!

Uh . . . Chief, it's the **Hong Kong Police!** I—I'm afraid it's **bad news!**
Did something happen to **McClod?**
No, to the **Hong Kong Police!** McClod wiped out **half the Police Force** with a **runaway fork-life truck!**
Hi, y'all! Wal, Chief, Ah'm ready fer my **next assignment!**
McClod, you're a **menace** to Police Forces the **world over!** You're not even going back to the **Meter Maids!** You're going to **sit behind a desk** and **address invitations** to the **Policeman's ball** till you **retire!**
Congratulations, Chief! You and the Marshal did such a **great job** busting **The Hong Kong Connection** that I've decided to **reward** you both!

Commissioner, you kin reward me by sendin' me back t' the wide open spaces of Tacos! I jest ain't the desk jockey type!
Grant him that, Sir, and you can consider that as MY reward, too!
Forget it! I've already rewarded McClod, by having him transferred to New York City PERMANENTLY!
. . . and since his unorthodox Western methods have proven so effective, I felt that a squad made up entirely of Cowboys would be a great way to fight crime in this Precinct! Chief Cliffhead . . . meet your new Police Department . . .
Hey, there yuh go!